D0674341

To Parents

The Ladybird **First Picture Dictionary** introduces children to letter shapes, letter sounds and alphabetical order – vital first steps in learning to read.

Here are some suggestions to help your child make the fullest use of this book:

* **The sound and word game** How many words can your child think of beginning, say, with the sound p… Turn to the letter p and see how many of these words are in the dictionary.

* **Test your memory** Choose a letter of the alphabet and spend several minutes looking at the words and pictures. Cover the pages. How many words can you and your child remember?

* **Find the word** Open the book and choose a word. Then close the book and ask your child to find it again. See if he or she can find it before you count to ten!

LINCOLNSHIRE
COUNTY COUNCIL

Published by Ladybird Books Ltd
80 Strand London WC2R 0RL
A Penguin Company

10

© LADYBIRD BOOKS LTD MCMXCIII This edition MCMXCIX

LADYBIRD and the device of a Ladybird are trademarks of Ladybird Books Ltd
All rights reserved. No part of this publication may be reproduced,
stored in a retrieval system, or transmitted in any form or by any
means, electronic, mechanical, photocopying, recording or otherwise,
without the prior consent of the copyright owner.

Printed in Italy

F•I•R•S•T
Picture
Dictionary

illustrated by GAYNOR BERRY

Ladybird

Aa

acrobat

anchor

aeroplane

apple

alligator

astronaut

Bb

ball

bird

banana

butterfly

basket

buttons

Cc

car

chair

castle

clock

cat

clown

Dd

digger

doll

dinosaur

drum

dog

duck

Ee

eagle

elephant

earrings

envelope

egg

explorer

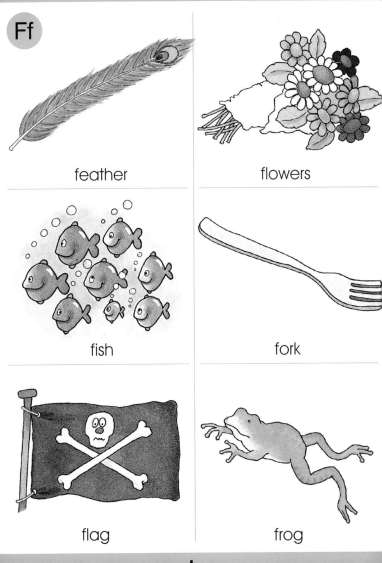

Ff

feather

flowers

fish

fork

flag

frog

Gg

garage

glass

gate

goat

ghost

guitar

Hh

hammer

helicopter

hands

horse

hat

house

Ii

ice cream

instruments

ink

iron

insect

island

Jj

jacket

jug

jam

juggler

jigsaw

jungle

Kk

kangaroo

knife

keys

knitting

king

koala

Ll

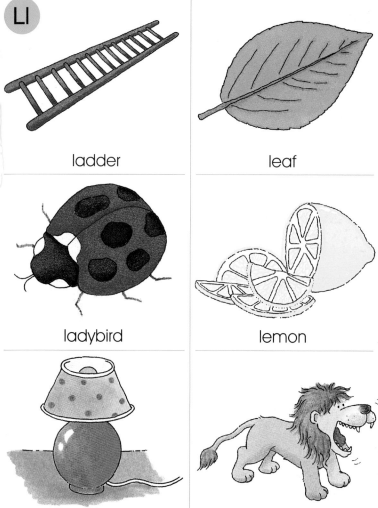

ladder

leaf

ladybird

lemon

lamp

lion

Mm

map

moon

mirror

mountain

monkey

mouse

Nn

necklace

net

needle

nurse

nest

nuts

Oo

octopus

ostrich

oil

oven

orange

owl

Pp

paint

penguin

palace

piano

pencil

pie

Qq

queen

question

quilt

Rr

rabbit

radio

rainbow

robot

Ss

sheep

rose

shoes

ruler

snake

Tt

spider

table

star

telephone

sun

television

tiger

train

tools

tree

tractor

trumpet

Uu

umbrella

unicorn

uniform

Vv

vegetables

violin

volcano

Ww

watch

whale

waterfall

wheels

web

wheelbarrow

whistle

woman

Xx

windmill

X-ray

wolf

xylophone

Yy

yogurt

Zz

zebra

yolk

zip

yo-yo

zoo

acrobat
aeroplane
alligator
anchor
apple
astronaut

ball
banana
basket
bird
butterfly

buttons

car
castle
cat
chair
clock
clown

digger
dinosaur
dog
doll
drum
duck

eagle
earrings
egg
elephant

envelope
explorer

feather
fish
flag
flowers
fork
frog

garage
gate
ghost
glass
goat
guitar

hammer
hands
hat
helicopter
horse
house

ice cream
ink
insect
instruments
iron
island

jacket
jam
jigsaw
jug
juggler
jungle

kangaroo
keys
king
knife
knitting
koala

ladder
ladybird
lamp
leaf
lemon
lion